G. Fauvel Gouraud

Ballads of coster-land

G. Fauvel Gouraud

Ballads of coster-land

ISBN/EAN: 9783744769556

Printed in Europe, USA, Canada, Australia, Japan

Cover: Foto ©Andreas Hilbeck / pixelio.de

More available books at **www.hansebooks.com**

BALLADS

OF

COSTER-LAND.

BY

G. FAUVEL GOURAUD.

New York:
Herald Square Publishing Co.
1897.

This book is dedicated
by the Author
"To his best Pal,"
(Col. Gouraud,)
"The Guv'ner."

PREFACE.

So many of my friends, who have heard me recite some of the verses contained in this collection, have asked why I did not publish them in book form, that I have at last decided to do so.

. For the benefit and information of those readers who do not know what a coster-monger is, a few words in explanation seem not to be amiss.

The costermonger is a sort of "hawker" or "peddler." He is seen in the suburbs of London and in the East End, selling flowers, fruit, etc. The donkey is, of course, a necessary adjunct to his outfit.

His characteristics and eccentricities are such as to almost constitute a distinctive species of the human race. He is unique in his language and his dress. The women also have a peculiar style of their own, especially as to headgear. Usually it is a large cloth hat with huge ostrich-feathers, of all colors, which have been given to them by sailors.

Mr. Albert Chevalier has done much to make this character both familiar to, and a favorite with, the public in this country.

G. F. G.

CONTENTS.

NOTE.

THE author begs to say that the following pieces are based upon stories told by Albert Chevalier and others, but for the first time written in verse:

" The Nipper and 'is Ma.
" The Nipper and the Cigar-stump."
" The Nipper and the Two Torfs."
" 'Ow Bill 'e got the Chuck."
" Tommy's Last Hours."

" 'Ow Bill, 'e got the Chuck."

"I 'LL tell yer 'ow it was, Sal,
   'Ow Bill, 'e got the chuck
   From out Sinte Paul's Cathedral ;
   'E never 'ad no luck."

" Me an' 'im went out awarkin'
   I showin' 'im the sights—
   'Im as never left the Boro'
   Not even Sunday nights.
   We went along through Luggit,
   An' was parsin' by the church,
   W'en Bill 'e stopped a sudding
   15

Looked round an' give a lurch.
An' said ter me surprised-like,
'Wot's that buildin'?' ter me says Bill.
'Dunno Sinte Paul's!' I arnserd,
'Sich ignerence mikes me ill.'
'Wot's Sinte Paul's?' ter me says Billy.
'It's a church,' ter 'im I cries ;
'A plice w'ere people wuships,
'An' culled Gawd's 'ouse o' prise.'
'Lor strike me pink !' says Billy,
'It's a plice I wants ter see ·
I'm goin' ter circumspect it
So come along o' me.'
'Garn,' sez I ter Billy,
'Let's come an' 'ave a wet.'
But wot's the good o' argyin'
W'en onct Bill's 'eart is set ?
So off Bill goes atrottin'
Up them cathedral steps,

An' off I goes a 'oppin'
An' 'as severeal wets."

" I 'ad three pots o' 'arf an' 'arf,
Took a puff from out me pipe,
Went out inter the street agin;
Gawd love me, wot a sight !
There was Bill a-sprawlin',
An' tumblin' on the ground ;
'Is langwidge it were orful,
'Twas 'eard fer miles around.
Sez I, ' Wot's up, me codger ?
Wot 'ave yer been an' done ?'
' W'y nofin',' arnswers Billy,
' But 'ad a bit o' fun."

" ' I went into the church,' says Bill,
' An' sees a lot o' blokes,
Some standin' up in boxes

Like them we 'as fer mokes.

I sees a bloomin' parthway

W'ich leads the hull way down

To a torf as was a-standin',

Togged out in a long w'ite gown

Jist like a bloomin' nightshirt.

Lor' lumme, did I ever

See a sight to beat it.

No, 'Arry, swelp me, never!'"

"'As no one took no notis,

I strolled around a bit,

Then up the bloomin' parthway,

Blow me, thought I'd 'ave a fit.

An' as I neared 'is Nightshirts,

'E looked up from off 'is book

An' said, "Good Gawd, 'ave mercy,

Else our souls will be forsook!"

Then ups I, an' sez : "Guv'ner

'Ere, wot's the bloomin' row?
Ain't yer never seen a coster?
Well, yer sees a smart 'un now."
Well, that there fairly knocks 'im.
'Is Nightshirts calls a bloke,
An' between 'em, ups an' outs me,
An' 'ere I am all broke.'

" Say, Sal, yer should a seen 'im :
'Is cloes tore orf 'is back,
'Is peepers shut, 'is boko bent,
An' in 'is skull a crack.
An' now 'e is a cripple,
An' swears no more 'e'll do
A church or a cathedral,
Strike 'im everlarstin' blue."

The Fairy o' Niagara.

"SAY, Bill, did I ever tell yer,"
　　Said 'Enery 'Awkins, M.P.,
"About that little fairy,
　　The neatest yer ever see?
It was w'en I were Attachy
　　An' guide ter 'Is Peacocks Li,
At the great Falls o' Niag'ra,
　　All arunnin' ter the sea."

"Naw, yer didn't," said Buffles, Esquire;
"But I'm willin' fer ter 'ear
　　Of 'er yer little fairy,

Of 'er yer little dear."
" Well, I will tell yer, Billy,"
Said 'Enery 'Awkins, M.P.,
At the great Falls o' Niag'ra,
Along o' Peacocks Li.

" She were the neatest donah,
O' flashin' gold 'er 'air,
'Er eyes like stars in 'eavin,
She were a treat fer fair.
'Er winnin' little ways, Bill,
'Twas lovely fer ter see,
W'en I were at Niag'ra,
Along o' Peacocks Li."

" Naw, I couldn't do 'er justice;
There ain't no words ter use
As would give yer a descripshun,
But yer'ld 'arf the pictshur lose;
She were a little haingel

The fust I ever see,
An' the great Falls o' Niag'ra
Kept arunnin' ter the sea."

" Now, Billy," said 'Enery 'Awkins,
" Jis' maike up yer bloomin' mind,
An' taike the fairest products
On earth as yer can find,
An' taike them all together,
There's none as fair as she,
That Fairy o' Niag'ra
A reg'ler haingel she."

The Nipper and the Cigar-stump.

WE 'ave a little nipper,
  A favrit down our way,
Went out ter do the Boro'
One Sattidy night larst May
'E was feelin' kind o' lonesome,
Gizin' serious all around,
An' 'e were on'y ten year old
An' four foot from the ground.

All at onct 'e stopped asudding,
Put 'is 'and up ter 'is brow,
Said, " Me nerves is out of order ;

I wonder wot's the row.
I've been suffrin' somethin' orful,
An' me 'ead is spinnin' round,"
Said this kid as were but ten year old
An' four foot from the ground.

'E stopped an' thought a minute,
Said, " 'Ere's a rummy joke!
W'y, since I seen me doctor
I 'aven't 'ad a smoke.
An' me who's fond o' baccy
Every week I smokes a pound,"
Said this kid as were but ten year old
An' four foot from the ground.

Jist then a torf come parsin' by,
Gorblimy, wot a terror
As 'e parsed 'e dropped 'is twofer—
A treat, no bloomin' error.

The nipper pounced upon it
As it lay there on the ground,
An' 'e were on'y ten year old
An' four foot from the ground.

Said the nipper as 'e held it,
" It smokes better w'en it's lit,
An' as I 'aven't got no match
I shall 'ave ter arsk fer it."
So 'e trots inter a 'bacconist,
Not dreamin' ter be downed,
Fer 'e were on'y ten year old
An' four foot from the ground.

Says the bloke be'ind the counter,
" We gives no lights away."
" Give over," says the nipper
" I'm willin' fer ter pay."
So 'e outs 'is on'y copper,—

Like a man 'e stood 'is ground,
An' 'e were on'y ten year old
An' four foot from the ground.

Said the nipper, " 'Ere, me codger,"
As 'e puffed 'is twofer stump,
" W'en a genelman arsks yer fer a light
Don't get the bloomin' 'ump,
But jist yer give 'im one o' mine
An' not a shabby throw-down,"
Said this kid as were but ten year old
An' four foot from the ground.

The Little Nipper an' 'is Ma.

"YER know me little nipper,"
  Said 'Enery 'Awkins, M.P.
Well, 'e's a little champion,
An' tikes on arfter me.
Larst Sunday me an' the missus
Went out fer a little walk—
I should say the nipper took us,
Yer should o' 'eard 'im tork!

"We went along through Tyburn,
  An' then by 'Endon way,
W'ere I ust ter do me courtin'

In those sweet nights o' May.
We'd been walkin' out an 'our,
W'en Sal she sez ter me,
"'Ere, 'Arry, is yer gime, dear,
Fer shrimps an' a cup o' tea.'

" 'Garn," sez I ter Sally,
" ' I'm in fer 'arf an' 'arf.'
Lor lumme, yer should jist o' 'eard
My little Sally larf!
'O' course,' she sez, ' I likes me nip
O' gin an' glarss o' beer,
But did not like ter say it out
Before the nipper 'ere.' "

" The nipper 'e warn't lookin'
As we neared the Brokers' Arms;
An' in we 'ops ter get a wet,
Not dreamin' any 'arm.

But the nipper 'e were cagy,
An' follered in the rear,
An' 'ears me give me order :
' 'Ere, miss, two pots o' beer.

" An' we'n I gives me order,
I turns ter speak ter Sal,
Ter arsk if she remembered
The day she was me gal.
I felt some one atuggin'
An' pullin at me back;
I looks around surprised-like,
An' sees that rascal Jack.

" Sez I, ' See 'ere, me nipper,
I wont 'ave yer 'angin' 'ere.'
Sez 'e, 'D'yer think I'm goin' ?
Not me.   No bally fear.
Now then, wot 'ave yer ordered ? '

Sez I, ' Two 'arf an' 'arf. '

Sez 'e, ' Ain't mother in it ? '

An' yer should o' 'eard 'im larf."

Tommy's Last hours, or his Reply to the Prison Chaplain.

" TELL us all about Tommy,"
  Me donah Sally she said.
" It's orful ter think of it, ain't it,
  Now poor old Tommy is dead ?"
" Yus, Sally, it is kind o' sadlike,
  But 'is ludship couldn't do naught
  Than say that Tommy were guilty,
  Seein' as 'ow 'e were caught
  Arunnin' away from the public,
  'Is togs all covered with blood,
  An' a knife concealed in 'is pocket,
  Though 'e did say, ' Not guilty, me lud.'"

31

" Say, 'Enery, didn't I 'ear yer
   Tell as 'ow you were by
   Poor old Tommy this mawrnin' ?
   Oh, 'Enery, I feels like a cry."
" Cheer up 'ere, Sally, me darlin',
   It ain't me as wot was strung up
   Dry yer peepers, Sally, and listen,
   An' I'll tell yer 'ow Tom 'e done up
   The parson as come ter the prisun
   Ter pray, fer ter save Tommy's soul,
   An' ter lead 'im up ter the gallers,
   An' ter plice 'im, w'en dead, in 'is ole.

" Well, Tommy were sittin' agizin'
   Around 'im in dull-like dispair;
   'Is peepers were bloody an' starin',
   An' 'e kep' apullin' 'is 'air.
   I standin' alone there beside 'im,
   A-tryin' to comfort an' cheer,

But no bally word did 'e give me
"'Cept, ' 'Enery, fetch me some beer.' "

" This were all 'e said, till the parson
Come in an' said, ' My good man,'
Which ups Tom, who 'ated sich codgers,
An' 'e swore as on'y 'e can.
But 'is Chaplains took it all calm-like,
An' down 'e plumped on 'is knee,
An' begun ter pray fer poor Tommas,
That 'is larst 'ours peaceful might be."

" Well, Tommy 'e stood it a minute,
An' said, ' 'Ere, 'ang it, old chap,
I warnts the larst 'ours by me lonesome,
Before they tries on the black cap.'
Again Tommy sat by 'is tible,
A 'oldin' 'is 'ands ter 'is 'ead,

An' the parson 'e kep' on a-prayin',
W'ile I sat down on the bed."

" W'en asudding I see Tommy standin'
Aglarin' around an' around,
An' 'is glarnce it lit on 'is Nightshirts
As 'e knelt there on the ground.
Then Tommy 'e yells somethin' orful,
An' calls the poor parson sich nimes,
An' the air turned as blue as the 'eavins,
Wot with blankety blanks an' Gorblimes.

" ''Ere, w'oo, strike me purple, are you, sir,
An' wot is yer doin' of 'ere ?'
' I'm the servant of Gawd, my good fel-
  low,
I pray, an' you need 'ave no fear.'
'Give over,' yells blasphemous Tommy,
' I wants no menials round 'ere.

I don't want yer gab an' yer prayers,
An' moreover I ain't got no fear.
So garn, give over,' yells Tommy.
' You've 'eard tell of a higher power,
You know w'om I mean—it's yer Guv'ner
W'om I'm goin' to meet in an 'our.' "

The Nipper an' the Two Torfs.

" ' ERE, guv'ner," said the nipper,
 W'en 'e come 'ome larst night,.
" I met two torfs this arternoon
 A-spoilin' fer a fight.
' We'll give yer 'arf a thick 'un,'
 The torfs ter me they said,
. ' If you will tike a piece o' mud
 An' 'it that copper's 'ead.' "

" ' Righto,' says I, ' I'll go yer one ;
 Out with the splosh,' sez I.
' Yer see that peeler standin' there ?
 See me 'it 'im in the heye.'

So ups I with a bit o' mud
An' 'its that cop a ripper
Right in the bloomin' peepers—
'Twas a fair one fer a nipper."

" 'Twas worth a 'arf a thick 'un
Ter see that bobby jump.
'E clapped 'is 'and up ter 'is brow
An' got the bloomin' 'ump ;
Fer strike me crimson if e't didn't
Nab the torfs an' me
An' runs us strite ter Bow Street !
Lorlumme, wot a spree !

" Then the bloke as writes the nimes down
Arsked one o' the torfs fer 'is un.
Said 'e, ' Yer'll 'ave ter give it,
Or else yer'll go ter prisun.'
That ups the torf, who arnsers,
' Lord Russell is me nime.'

' Lor strike me pink,' the bloke sez,
' 'Ere's a pretty gime !' "

" Then 'e turns an' arsks the Hother,
' Wot may your nime be ?'
' I'm 'is Grice the Duke o' Norfolk,'
The torf ter 'im says 'e.
Well, that there fairly knockea 'ım
As 'e writ it in 'is book.
'E were silent 'arf a minute,
'E seemed afeared ter look."

" Then 'e turns an' sez, ' 'Ere, youngster,
Wot's yer bloomin' nime ?
Don't give me any spoofin',
Or put up any gime.'
' Righto,' says I, outspoken,
' I'm not roundin' on me pals,
Fer I'm Sir Billiam 'Arcourt,
An' a terror with the gals.' "

La Loie Fuller.

" SAY, Bill, 'ave yer seen Loie Fuller?"
    Said 'Enery 'Awkins, M.P.,
  Ter 'is pal Billiam Buffles, Esquire,
  O' Whitechapel Road, E. C.
" Tell yer wot, she's a terror at darncin';
  Maikes yer 'air curl up with delight,
  Sends the blood rushin' through yer hull
    systim,
  As yer gaize on 'er togged out in w'ite."
" Naw, I 'aven't," says Buffles, Esquire,
" I never goes ter the play;
  An' wot's more, I likes Flossy's darncin',

Wot I could watch the hull day."
" Garn with yer gab," then cries 'Awkins,
" Yer dunno yer own bloomin' min'
W'y, tork about hingels in 'eavin,
Their darncin' ain't nigh so sublime
As the steps as wot Loie Fuller
Does at the 'All on the staige.
If yer like I'll tell yer about 'er,
Fer blow me if she ain't the raige."

" She fust comes on togged out in flimses
O' black, 'er 'air all a-curl,
An' she glides' cross the staige all a-blazin',
W'ich sets yer brain in a whurl;
An' then with the crimson an' yeller,
The blue an' the green an' w'ite,
Yer'ld think as 'ow it were magic
As yer see the staige dark, then light.
'La Fervelent' is wot she calls it,

Wot means the moon and the sun,
The stars an' the hull bloomin' 'eavin .
Altergether jobbed up inter one."

" Then she 'as wot gives yer the shudders,
An' put yer 'and ter yer eyes
Fer fear yer'ld see 'er a-blazin'
In flames which gives yer surprise.
Lor' lumme, Bill, did I ever
See hanythink like it afore!
I gives it yer streight, it's a terrer,
I'm agoin' ter see it onct more.
The flames is green and then crimson,
Then they chinges ter every 'ue,
Jist like a 'ouse all afire,
An' yer claps till yer 'ands is all blue."
" An' 'er larst one, no doubt about it,
Is a knockout, a fair bloomin' treat;
She calls it the ' Toolip ' or ' Lily.'

I'll tell yer it's 'ard fer ter beat.

When she darnces it, twelve bloomin'
　　mirrers

Are exposed ter the view o' the 'ouse,

An' the music plays softly and gently;

We blokes is as still as a mouse.

She runs round the staige like a phantim,

'Erself in the mirrers yer see,

Which maikes it seem as if fifty

Were trying ter copy ' Loie.'

Now farster she runs and farster,

'Er dress all sailin' around,

An' the lights is givin' their colers

From the sides, the top, and the ground.

Then asudding she stops in the centre,

An' waives 'er arms in the air,

An' white lights blaize all around 'er—

It's a straight old knockout fer fair.

Then she spins and then spins all a-flashin'

In the lights, which maikes 'er appear
Fust like an hangel from 'eavin,
With fifty more in the rear,
Then like a butiful flower
As couldn't be found down our way.
But the rub is, it larsts but a minute,
Instead of all night and all day."

" 'Ere,'Enery," says Buffles, Esquire,
"I'll go, if wot's yer've said's true;
An' wot's more, I'll pay fer yer ticket.
We'll taike Liza and Floss along too."
" Right yer are," says 'Enery 'Awkins,
" I'm glad ter see as yer've sense.
We go every night, that she's darncin'
An' 'ang it all, blow the expense !"

The Nipper's Spoof.

"SALLY, I fears that 'e's goin',
    I sees a queer look in 'is eyes,
Oh, Sally, see 'im there pantin',
    An' the red spot wot on 'is cheeks lies !
Oh, Sally, wot shall we be doin'
    Without our nipper around,
W'en we've laid 'im out in 'is corfin,
    An' put 'im down in the ground ?"

" Don't tork like that, 'Enery darlin',
    Me 'eart is bally near bust;
I carnt bear ter see 'im there diein',
44

I wish that I might go fust.
Fer ter think that we carnt do nofin'
But watch our little kid go—
It's orful, 'Enery, so 'elp me ! "
An' Sal's tears begun fer ter flow."

Sal's anguish were orful ter witness ;
She yelled 'an she tore at 'er 'air,
An' 'Enery sat watchin' the nipper
An' rockin' about in dispair.

At larst the nipper 'e opened
'Is eyes an' look all around
An' said, " 'Ere, guv'ner, old pally,
I'll soon be laid in the ground.
Jist tike good care of yer Sally ,
Be kind ; she's me mother, yer know.
An,' mother, be good ter the guv'ner,
Fer yer see I've got fer ter go."

" Oh, dontcher tork like that, Jacky,"
   Sally, a-blubbin', she said ;
" Yer ain't goin' ter leave us just yet, dear."
   An' she went and knelt down by the bed,
   An' took the kid's thin 'and an' pressed
     it,
   An' kissed the poor nipper's red fice ;
   An' 'Enery 'e jist stood a-watchin',
   An' never moved from 'is plice.

———

" Good-by ; I'm agoin', I knows it.
   Kiss me, guv'ner, quick now, old pal.
   An' you too, mover ; 'ere, 'urry,
   I feels meself goin,' old gal."
   An' strong-'earted 'Enery 'e kissed 'im,
   An' Sal she fell ter the ground ;
   Fer they thought the nipper'd stopped
     torkin'
   Till the world 'ad ceased goin' around.

They was weepin' their heyes out in an-
     guish,
Sal jolly near went in a fit,
W'en the nipper 'e uped an' 'e 'ollered,
" W'y, I ain't nearly dead yit.
     'Ere, wot er yer gittin' at, Sally?
I were on'y doin' a spoof.
An,' guv'ner, me comps ter the doctor,
An' jist yer fork out some oof."

Well, tork about bein' knocked silly
An' bein' tiken aback !
The nipper 'e did 'isself proud, sir;
An' 'Awkins sez, " Look 'ere, young Jack,
If hever I catches yer spoofin',
If hever yer tries on this gime,
Sal an' me will disown yer, me nipper,
     An' yer'll 'ave ter tike on a new nime."

Well, the nipper 'e soon calmed 'em over,
Fer they was proud o' their boy,
Fer 'e was their fust an' their on'y,
An' a source o' care an' o' joy.
E' were allus gittin' in pickles,
A-comin' 'ome 'wi some tile
O' 'ow 'e'd done up another,
Else a peeler 'e'd managed to rile.

'Awkins in New York.

THE following verses have been written
by special request.

They tell of a few of 'Enery 'Awkins's
adventures during his supposed visit to New
York after having left Li Hung Chang,
whom he had met in London and accom-
panied to the United States. Parts I and
II are supposed to be told by him on his
return to London. Parts III and IV are
told colloquially.

The author begs to offer his apologies to
the Honorable Chauncey M. Depew for
the liberty he has taken in using his name
in these verses.

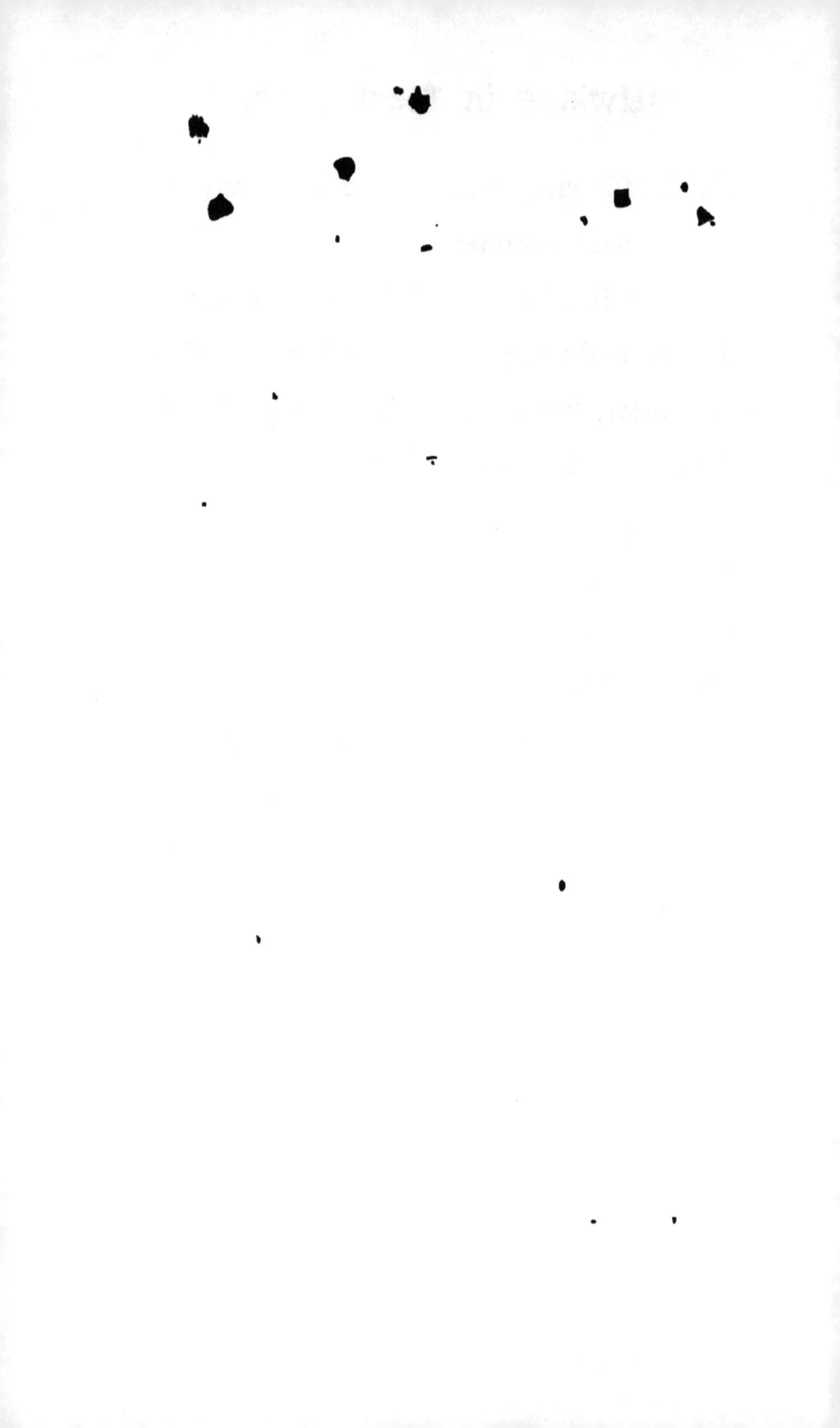

Part I.

'AWKINS AT THE WALDORF

AND ON THE BOWERY.

51

I.

"Wotcher me, pals," said 'Enery 'Awkins,
Ter us all the night 'e come back
From Hamericy. There were that even-
　　ing
Buffles, an' Morgin, an' Jack
Wot's married to 'Enery's sister,
An' Tomus o' Hammersmith Road,
An' 'Enery w'ose larst nime is Muggins,
An' Bill Foster, nicknamed " The Toad."
We was all o' us at the Blue Dragon,
A-drinkin' o' 'Awkins' good 'ealth ;
'E'd jist come back from a wisit
Ter New York, w'ere 'e'd mide some
　　pelf.
Blow me, 'e were togged out dossy

A 'igh 'at, a stick, an' a coller,

And gloves mide o' kid, no darn errer;

'Is tie would o' mide the Prince 'oller;

An' trotters as shone like a mirrer,

An' pinched 'is poor bloomin' toes,

They was pinted like toothpicks, yus,
    blow me;

An' lor' e' did 'ave sich clothes!

II.

Well, Enery said, "'Ere, now, you codg·
    ers,

I'll tell yer all of me trip

In the land o' the Free an' the Bowery,

Wot is on'y reached in a ship.

Yer knows 'ow I went wi' the Viceroy,

Wot is better known as Earl Li;

'E's wot they call on the Bowery

A ' Chink ' or a ' 'eathen Chinee.'

III.

‘ Well, I left ’im w’en ’e sailed fer China,

An’ went ter New York on me own,

An’ stayed at the lovliest public.

(Yus, Tomus, I were alone.)

Well, this public, they calls it the Wal-
dorf—

An’ blow me, tork of yer style !

It’s a treat, no bloomin’ errer.

(’Ow ’igh ? Well, nearly a mile.)

But the food that they gives yer ! Well,
really,

They ain’t got a thing fit ter eat

Not even a bloomin’ red ’errin’;

An’ as fer pickled pig’s feet,

W’y, blow me, they rook yer a fortune;

An’ they cost me near ’arf a crown.

Fer a bed they arsks 'arf a thickun,
An' a tanner each time yer looks round.

IV.

" Then wun night I was 'avin' some supper,
An' a bloke called Chauncey Depew
Come up an' said, ' 'Enery 'Awkins,
I likes yer, well, jist a few.'
(Who's Chauncey ?   Well, now yer jist
        knocks me.
W'y, 'e's wot they calls ' a real peach '—
Wot is slang fer callin' a codger
The on'y real stone on the beach.)
Well, Chauncey 'e says ter me, ' 'Enery,
'Ow would yer like fer ter go
Along 'o me an' a codger
Whom I'd like yer now fer ter know ?
We'll go an' run round the Bowery—
Yer've 'eard me speak of that plice;

We'll also go wisit some cafys
Wot I tells yer is orfully nice.'

V.

" ' I'm with yer, Chauncey, no errer;
Yer does me proud, me dear boy.'
Then he knocks me down to a codger
Wot mide me dizzy wi' joy;
Fer Chauncey 'e said 'e were really
A bloke wot 'ad so much oof
Wot if laid out in fivers would cover
Old Hengland an' Ireland—no spoof.

VI.

" Well, we jumps in a chise culled a landy,
Chauncey, this codger, an' me,
An' started ter do up the Bowery,
An', blow me, we did 'ave a spree !

Fust we drives down a road they calls
    Broadway—
Gawd love yer, it ain't arf as wide
As a halley down in the Boro',
Yet they calls it ' Americy's Pride.'
All along yer sees blokes arunnin'
An' tearin' an' cuttin' about,
Ter try an' get out of the way of
The trams.   'Ow they shout
Ter get those trams ter a standstill!
W'y, would yer believe w'en I say
That w'en one stops fer a minute
It's writ up in the paipers next day?

VII.

" Well, at larst we got ter the Bowery.
    On the way there warn't much ter see
    Till we got ter a plice called Steve Brodies

W'ere we 'ad a drink o' cold tea.

Leastways that's wot Chauncey 'e told
me.

(Did I like it? No bloomin' fear.

Fer, blow me, give me the ' Dragon '

With yer gin an' yer pint o' good beer.)

Well, Chauncey 'e said ter me, ' 'Enery,

Mister Brodie 'e' is a grite chap,

'E'll jump from a bridge 'igh as 'eaven

An' on the way down tike a nap.'

' Give over,' says I ter 'is Peachlets,

· Don't give me none o' yer spoof.'

' That's right,' answers quickly old Chauncey,

' That's 'ow 'e mikes all 'is oof.'

VIII.

" Well, boys, yer'ld never o' thought it,

But then yer knows it's New York

W'ere people does things as is crizy,
An' Lor', 'ow some o' them tork !

IX.

" The next thing we sees were a caffy.
Yer pays nofin' at all ter go in
(They've singin' jist like at the Royal),
But Lor', 'ow they soaks yer fer gin !
But Chauncey 'e says, ' Never mind it,
I'm puttin' up all o' the dough.'
(Wot's dough ?   Well, there, 'Enery Mug-
    gins,
It's oof or splosh, doncher know.)
Soon Chauncey 'e says ter me, ' 'Enery,
Ain't that a bird on the stige !
Lor', wot eyes, wot a figger ! '
Says I ter 'im, ' Chaunce, you'll oblige
If yer'll tell me wot ever ye're arfter.
I sees no bird in the plice.'

Well, Chauncey 'e larfed an' 'e arnswered.
' Well, 'Enery, you do cut the ice.'

X.

" Now, boys, yer tork o' yer lingos,
    Well, that wot they use in New York
    It beats all I've 'eard in the Boro'.
    Blow me, 'ow rummy they tork !

XI.

" Soon we leaves the caffe, as the poet
    'E says, fer fields wot is new,
    Me an' the millyingaire codger
    An' 'is Peachlets Chauncey Depew.

Part II.

'AWKINS IN CHINATOWN.

" When we left the Bowery
We went through Chinatown;
We met the grite Chuck Connors,
A bloke o' grite renown.
'E lives among the Chinee
An' mikes 'em all 'is pals;
An' fer fighten' 'e's a terrer,
An' a fav'rit with the gals."

II.

" We 'ad a wet called Sam Shu
An' a mess they called Chow Dong,
An' met a bloke called Ski Hi
An' another called Bing Bong.

Yer never 'eard sich torkin',
'Twere like a lot o' geese,
It were really somethin'k orful,
An' I 'ad ter cry fer peace."

III.

" But Chaunce 'e seemed ter like it;
They bowed and bowed agin,
An' arsked 'im fer ter jine 'em
In a glass o' Chinese gin.
We sat down ter the tible,
They give us lots, o' stuff;
Our pal 'as 'ad the ooftish
At it on'y mide a bluff."

IV.

"Then a bloke as 'ad a pigtail—
(Wot's a pigtail?   Well, I never!
Ain't yer never 'eard o' pigtails?

Sich ignerence! Swelp me ever!
W'y, a pigtail is a lot o' 'air
A 'angin' down yer back;
Some reaches right down ter the ground,
An' others 'arf way back.)

v

" Well, as I said, a codger
Got up and said, ' Dear Chaunce,
Won't yer let us 'ave some torkin',
Or would yer like ter dawnce?'
Then Chaunce 'e ups an' bows a bit,
An' puffs 'is 'uge segar,
An' says, ' Before I speechifies
We'll 'ave ter 'it the bar.' "

VI.

" So they goes an' fills the glarsses,
An' Chaunce 'e raises 'is

An' says, ' Me pals an' comrades,
Let's drink in this 'ere fizz
The 'ealth of 'Enry 'Awkins,
The on'y pebble on the beach,
An' the 'ealth o' me, the on'y,
The grite and on'y Peach.' "

VII.

" Sich shoutin' an' 'urrahin'
Yer ne'er afore did 'ear ;
The Chinks they yelled out, ' Blava ! '
W'ile I yells out, ' 'Ear 'ear ! '
An' Chaunce an' t'other codger
They fairly jumps wi' glee
Ter 'ear the grite ovation
O' these rummy old Chinee."

VIII.

" Then a bloke all togged in satin
O' green an' blue an' red

Gits up an' bows perlite like,
An' then ter Chaunce 'e said,
' Me noble comlade Chauncee,
Me muchee likee you,
Me likee 'Enly 'Awkins,
Yas, belly much a few.'

IX.

" Then 'e arsked us all ter jine 'im
An' 'ave a little gime—
The bloke 'e called it Fan Tan
Or some sich bloomin' nime;
But Chaunce 'e threw 'is 'ands up
An' cried, ' Oh, nottee me,
I playee only baccalat,
Like me pal the Plince, yer see.' "

Part III.

'AWKINS AN' THE BOWERY GIRL.

I.

'Enry 'Awkins went out walking
Not so very long ago,
Before he left America—
At least they tell me so.

II.

He'd been in New York City
About a week or two,
And there really wasn't anything
Left for 'Awkins now to do.

III.

But one night he sat a-thinking
And wondering what to do;

Said he, " I'll tike a little stroll
Along Third Avenoo."

IV.

" Fer I'd like ter 'ave some flirtin'.
I wants ter meet a gal,
A regler out-an'-outer,
Like me little donah Sal."

V.

He soon had reached the Bowery,
When he spied a maiden swell
Who, as he neared, cried out to him,
" Say, youse dinky mug, what t' 'ell ! "

VI.

Poor 'Awkins was astonished
To hear this lingo queer,

But he braces up and says, " Old gal,
Let's go an' 'ave some beer."

VII.

" Say, English," cried the hoyden,
" Does youse mean it on de dead,
  Or is youse only bluffin'?"
  Said 'Awkins, " Strike me red !"

VIII.

" Strike you red?   What yer givin' us ?
  Strike yer nothun.   I don't think
  I'll strike youse fer er ten-spot
  When youse blown me ter er drink."

IX.

She led the way, and 'Awkins
Meekly followed by her side;

And they entered what she called a
 "cafe,"
And she to the waiter cried,

X.

" Say, youse mug, come get a gait,
For me gentleman fren' and me
Ain't got no time to monkey.
Two up, me cully, see ?"

XI.

The waiter brought the beer, and then
As 'Awkins drank he said,
" Lor' lumme, call this beer ?
Well there, 'ere strike me dead."

XII.

" What t' 'ell ! " the damsel softly cried.
' Say, don't yer trun no bluff;

Dis beer ain't no mixed ale, see ?
It's de genuine real stuff."

XIII.

" Lor' luv yer, gal," then 'Awkins cried,
" Yer is a treat, no errer.
I luv yer, swelp me bob, I does !
Yer is a regler terrer."

XIV.

" Say, what youse mean, you English dude,
Is youse talkin' on de level ?
Ain't youse tryin' fer ter pull me leg ?
Say, youse is a sassy devel."

XV.

" Yus, on the straight. Say, wot's yer
     nime,
An' wot's yer occupashun ?

Fer, swelp me, gal, I likes yer, yas,
An' yer gives me palpitashun."

XVI.

" Me name is Hatpin Nellie, see ?
I'm the Champeen of the Bowery.
Me occupation it is nit;
An' me mother was a loidy."

XVII.

Then 'Enry 'Awkins to her said,
" I am a coster poet
An' lite attatchy ter Earl Li."
Cried Nellie, " Say, there, stow it !"

XVIII.

" You ain't so warm, me buty, see ?
I am as warm as you.

I'll be yer steady, if youse like,
For I luves yer jist a few."

XIX.

But sad, alas! it is to tell:
A great big burly brute
Arrived, and fired poor 'Awkins out
With the end of his hobnail boot.

XX.

For he was what is known down there
As Hatpin Nellie's steady,
And 'Awkins swore he'd ne'er return,
Not for thousands of the ready.

Part IV.

'AWKINS AT THE OPERA.

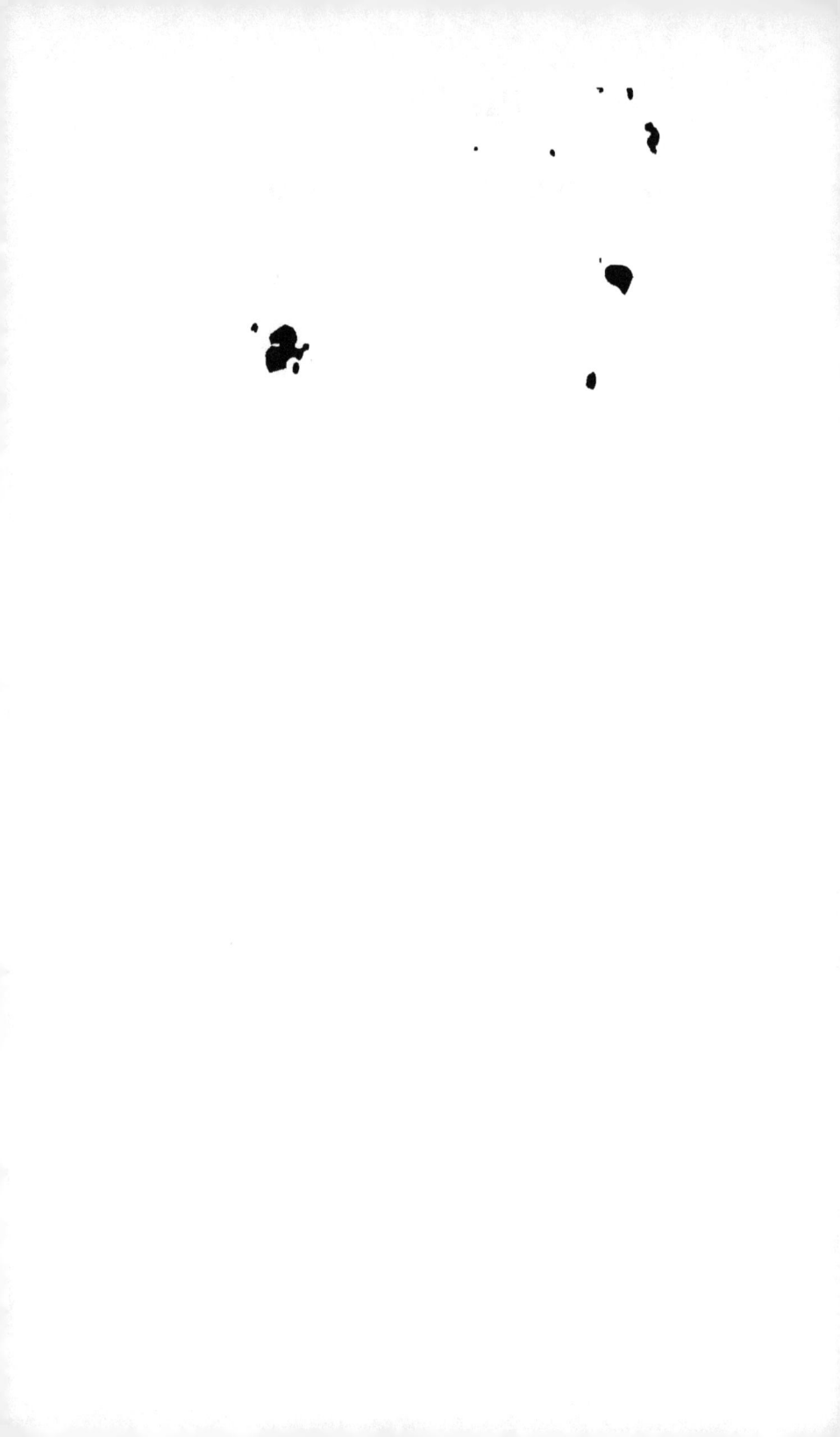

I.

" I say, 'Enery 'Awkins," said Chauncey
   Depew,
  One night while sitting at dinner,
" Would you like to go to the opera, me boy,
  With me and a regular winner ? "

II.

" Righto, me dear boy," 'Enery 'Awkins re-
   plied,
" I ll go yer one, so'elp me never.
  There's nofin I likes like Opery Grand,
  Though I rarely goes, leastways 'ardly
   ever."

III.

So they get in a chaise that was waiting
    without—
'Enery 'Awkins, dear Chaunce, and the
    Winner.
(A winner, I'm told, is a damosel fair
Who could make an old saint turn a
    sinner.)

IV.

They soon reached the home of Opera
    Grand,
Where they were then singing *Fav'rita*.
When 'Awkins he saw Madame Melba
    he cried,
" Gawd luv me, I'd like fer ter meet 'er ! "

V.

Cried Chauncey, "You shall; she's a great
    pal of mine.
I'll ask her to join us here later."
And 'Awkins replied, "Yer rumbo, me
    boy,
Yer ain't no bloomin' 'arf-rater."

VI.

Then 'Awkins looked round and inspected
    the girls,
Who were there to be seen, not to see,
And said to Depew, "O Chauncey, me
    pal,
Ah there! goodness gracious! oh me!"

VII.

"Did yer ever in all of yer hull bloomin' life
See in public gals' frocks cut so low?

I never did, I'll give yer that straight.
Why do they ? You ought ter know."

VIII.

" Well, really, dear 'Enery," said Chauncey
    Depew,
" Ask me, please, something more simple.
    It may be to show some radiant charm,
    A white snowy neck or a dimple."

IX.

" Yer don't tell me so! " said 'Awkins, M.P.
" On the crump they're barmy, I'm thinkin';
    Leastways they 'ad togged 'emselves out
        in a rush,
    Though they seems ter 'ave spent some
        time prinkin'."

X.

" Say, Chaunce, who is that with a bloomin,
   red beard,
An' 'air wot is black as a nigger's
An' wot seems ter me ain't never been
   cut ?
W'y, if mine were like that I'ld 'ave jig-
   gers."

XI.

" That, my dear boy is a very nice chap,
   A jolly good sort of a fellow;
He's a Senator, fierce with his tawny lion's
   mane."
'Awkins muttered aloud, " Strike me yel-
   low ! "

XII.

"Well, yas," added 'Awkins, "'e do strike
 me so
"An' ain't 'e a rather 'igh liver?"
"I don't know about that," answered
 Chauncey Depew,
"But he *is* a great dinner-giver."

XIII.

"An' w'o is the chap wot is standin' up there
 Like a monick of all he surways?"
"That" said Depew is "Please-look-at-me-
 do!
Whom no one is able to phaze."

XIV.

"W'o is that bloke with a crutch an' one
 leg,
"Wot is 'obblin' down the right aisle?"

"That, my dear boy, is a warrior brave,
   A terrible man, sir, to rile."

XV.

" An' 'ow did 'e lose 'is poor bloomin' leg ?"
" At Gettysburg," was the reply;
" And in taking it off he chewed at his weed
   And only gave vent to a sigh."

XVI.

" An' w'o is that bloke wot looks like a
      duke,
   Or else like a noble 'ussar ?
   'E looks as if 'e an army might lead,
   Even stampede a hull church bazar."

XVII.

"He, my dear sir, is known the world o'er
   And you tell me you don't know his
      name.

He is the Grand Marshal of every parade,
And is ever increasing his fame."

XVIII.

And so he went on, did 'Awkins, M.P.,
With questions and questions galore,
Till Chauncey cried, " Halt, O 'Enery, do,
My throat is gettin' quite sore."

XIX.

" Wot, Chauncey, me peach, does I 'ear yer
      correct,
Does I 'ear yer rightly, me boy—
That yer tired o' 'earin' yer own little voice,
Wot is every one's pleasure an' joy?"

XX.

" Yes, really I'm tired, and I beg to say
      here
It is a remarkable fact,

That some people say that my jokes are
　　moss-grown
And that 'I am losin' my tact."

XXI.

" Oh no, it's not true," answered 'Awkins,
　　M.P.
" You're the idol of every child,
　Ter say nofin' of womin an' also the men;
　Yer a Peach, an' that's drawin' it mild."

XXII.

Just then there arose a wondrous cheer,
Like the roar of the waves on the beach;
For the people had seen for the first time
　　that night
The Honorable Doctor de Peach.

XXIII.

And as the cheers ceased, 'Enery 'Awkins
  he said,
"Yer see, me dear boy, I were right;
  They luvs yer all still, I gives it yer
    straight,
  Yer are a bit of all right."

Vocabulary.

Arf an' 'arf, half beer and half porter.
'Arf a thickun, half a sovereign (about $2.50).
Barmy on the crump, a little crazy; queer.
Bloke, a person.
Bloomin' 'ump, to get sulky.
Blubbin', crying.
Boko, nose.
Cagy, sly, artful.
Chuck, the, to throw out, expel.
Codger, a fellow.
Corfin, coffin.
Donah, a sweetheart.
Downed, to be, to be disappointed.
Fivers, five-pound notes.
Flimses, laces, loose flowing gowns, etc.
Garn, go on.
Hull, whole.
Knock 'em, astonished them.
Jobbed up into one, all mixed together.
Lor lumme, the Lord love me.
Lingo, language.
Moke, donkey.

93

Nipper, a small boy.

Ooftish, money.

Peepers, eyes.

Peacocks Li, His Excellency Li Hung Chang.

Peeler, a policeman.

Public, a saloon.

Rooks yer fer gin, charge you for a glass of gin.

Rummy, queer, odd.

Rumbo, you're, you're a good sort of a fellow ; you are all right.

Soaks yer fer gin, charge you, etc.

Spoof, a bluff, a trick.

Splosh, money.

Torf, a swell, dude.

Twofer, two cigars for a penny (two cents).

Trotters, boots.

Tanner, sixpence (about 12 cents).

The Royal, a music-hall in the east end of London.

Wet, a drink.

www.ingramcontent.com/pod-product-compliance
Lightning Source LLC
Chambersburg PA
CBHW021419090426
42742CB00009B/1185